AF584736

POETRY by JAMES HUMPHREY

After I'm Dead,
Will My Life Begin? (1986) Volume

In Tribute To Survivors (1984) Chapbook

In New York City Air (1984) Chapbook

The 5¢ Poem (1981) Chapbook

The Re-Learning (1976) Volume

An Homage: The End
Of Some More Land (1972) Chapbook

The Visitor (1972) Chapbook

Argument For Love (1970) Volume

AFTER I'M DEAD, WILL MY LIFE BEGIN?

P o e m s B y

James Humphrey

POETS ALIVE! PRESS
Harrisburg, North Carolina
1986

AFTER I'M DEAD, WILL MY LIFE BEGIN?

Special thanks to the editors of the following magazines for publishing or accepting for publication, many of these poems: *The Arts Journal* (North Carolina), *Bertie Ledger-Advance, Black Bear, Bitterroot, Coraddi, Crescent Observer, Cutbank, East 149th Street Subway Station Writers Bench, The Fiddlehead* (University of New Brunswick, Canada), *Front Street Trolley, Grand Street, Gravity Cafe, Ink, Lips, Maat, Mill Hunk Herald, New Voices, No Magazine, Ohio Review, Oyez Review, The Panhandler, Poetry Now, Poets & Booze, Rhode Island Review, River City Review, The Round Table, Scree, The Small Pond Magazine of Literature, Stone Country, The Sun* (Chapel Hill, North Carolina), *Swift Kick, Taurus, Visual Showcase 2, West End.*

STILL TRYING originally appeared in *Manhattan Poetry Review* in a somewhat different form. FOR MAY VAN VOOREN, *Died 1979*, originally appeared in *Up Against The Wall, Mother*...in a somewhat different form.

Some of these poems were read on *National Public Radio,* Bob Edwards, host, Washington, D.C., WFDD-FM, Wake Forest University, Peter Dean, host, Winston-Salem, North Carolina, *Night Flight, WJR, Jay Roberts, host, Detroit, Michigan.*

Some of these poems appeared in the chapbooks *The 5¢ Poem, In New York City Air: For Ted Berrigan, In Tribute To Survivors,* copyright © 1981, 1984 by James Humphrey and Saroyan Humphrey.

Book Dedication quote from the song *Octopus's Garden,* written by Richard Starkey (Ringo Starr), copyright Starling Music Inc., BMI, 1969. Reprinted by permission. The song is on the album *The Beatles, 1967-1970.*

Book dedication poem *Hot, Hot Soup* was written by Monica Sawyer, fourth grade student (1985-86), Lawrence Academy, Merry Hill, North Carolina. Reprinted by permission.
Adrienne Rich quote in the poem *For My Son Saroyan, On His High School Graduation, May 31st, 1984, Greensboro, North Carolina* is from her lecture *Blood, Bread and Poetry: The Location of the Poet,* given at The University of Massachusetts-Amherst, September 28, 1983, published in *The Massachusetts Review*, Volume 24, Number 3, Autumn, '83, copyright c 1983 by Adrienne Rich. Reprinted by permission.

After I'm Dead, Will My Life Begin?, was printed January, 1986 for the Poets Alive! Press by the Edwards & Broughton Company, Raleigh, North Carolina, on permanent paper.

There are 2,000 books in this First printing.

LIBRARY OF CONGRESS CATALOGING IN PUBLICATION DATA

Humphrey, James, 1939-
After I'm Dead, Will My Life Begin?

I. Title
PS3558.U446A69   1986   811'.54   86-76
ISBN 0-936641-00-2 (permanent paper) (soft cover)

For My Son Saroyan,
with Deepest Love,
Highest Respect

Oh what joy for every girl and boy,
knowing they are happy and safe

-from *Octopus's Garden*,
by Richard Starkey

Hot, Hot soup
wonderful in
a blue bowl!

A poor child
eats the soup
on a cold
winter day,
licking the bowl
until it is clean.

Monica Sawyer,
grade 4

Table of Contents

After I'm Dead, Will My Life Begin?

SPRING, '84

Dogged winter wants
way indefenitely. Third
straight in heatless

house, cold, damp,
mold grows on walls,
ceiling.

Last seven weeks, *All*
of spine Violent
Pain! Arms, legs,

barely move. Harder
now to not be
cruel to self as

stepfather was. He,
Sadistic, mother
passive, watched him

bind my arms, legs,
throw me into lake
450 feet deep, both

left. Saved by only
sister, and she
couldn't swim!

Several times a week,
beaten, kicked in
stomach, groin, spine.

Locked in windowless
cellar, chained, tortured.
Permanent knife wounds.

Made to run
in dark, chased with
loaded gun. Shot at.

Don't remember being
called by real name.
"Shit Face" was one

spoken most. *Always,*
accomplishments degraded,
constantly told

never would amount
to anything: *first*
memories, ages four

to eleven. All these
years Trying, *Again,*
Again, from poverty's

skeleton, perpetually
in sight of what's
better. Body now

wants to give in,
end. I know
all of it

meaningless pain,
suffering; want spring
to overtake me before

summer's humidity heavily
bullies in, destroys
any chance

late arriving spring has
to open heart, keep
it trying.

DEEP WINTER POEM

For Norma & Our Son Saroyan

Winter-bared fingers
trying to split
grey clouds.

Glimmers of apparitions:

Weathered woman,
arms open,

man,
kind to their children.

Children,

not afraid.

Anthem

of my heart:

Fathers, Mothers everywhere,

be this

and live.

IN THE MOUTH OF THE DEVIL

Norma, Saroyan and I rent this decaying
cracker box near the closed
cotton mill.
Hundreds of houses identical
surround it.
One floor on cement blocks,
four tiny rooms of peeling
wallpaper over thin, crumbling
plaster board busted through
from too many raging fists.
In one of them facing the street,
I write, read what helps me
stay in the ring of risk, of
sacrifice, of wanting to live,
wanting to write.

My neighbors, young white males
and females laid off from the mill
when it shut down four years ago,
sit on worn-out tires and
broken chairs in dirt yards
of urine smells,
drinking warm beer, cheap wine,
a half-dozen single speaker radios
blaring AM rock from each side
of the street, trying to be louder
and louder.

They believe they are right.
They believe they are stronger
than I am.
They beleive they will win.

I continue in the ring of risk
and drag their dead dogs
from the street and bury them.

RECOVERING ALCOHOLIC

For Myself

Abandoned as
bus depot moth
dead on tile floor
in corner
next to public crapper.

Again,
talking to self
without success,
tapping foot
to no time.

Moving aimlessly
in tighter and
tighter circle.

> Here, in
> it, how
> to see this
> is *NOT* ALL,
>
> *NOT* EVERYTHING,
> Forever?

Not first time
in this fix, Buddy.
Give self credit
for no longer drinking,
for lasting, *not*

giving in to
alcohol's final
humiliation, Lucifer's
laughter destroying spirit.

LISTEN

Americans
are
obsessed
with
digging
out
a
meaning
first
time
through
a
poem
If
not
found
it
is
thrown
out
for
no
good
or
too
complicated
What's
wrong
with
"only"
having
emotional
response
with
poem
Each
of
us
poet
or
not
remembers

longer
feelings
about
something
than
meaning

LUCKY ME
IN COMFORTABLE HOUSE

For Bob, Penelope, Willy & Hannah Creeley

First morning sunlight
reaches this window.
This time

I'm here too
in it, putting
words on paper.

Too early for
children's voices
reaching up

from sidewalk.
Perfect silence
brings out soft,

rare memory.
Brookings, South
Dakota, in new

snow, I was 12,
she smiled *at me.*
This day,

a perfect beginning.

THIS DAY HAS SUNG TO ITSELF

Afternoon, 2:15, January
25th, becoming bright grey

after four straight days,
nights fierce sleet.

Street deserted except
guy in wheelchair, legs

amputated near groin, one
arm; jeans, sweatshirt, red

bandanna around neck,
hand turning wheel like

crazy! SPINNING! SPINNING!
GRINNING AND GRINNING!

POETS, REMEMBER TO PLAY

Pleasant sitting here
in university library carrel,
warm, easy to give into

buoyancy of light,
pleasurable sleep. Mind
won't focus, wants to

drift.

Out window,
two janitors, one
walks with mop

over shoulder, other
wheels bucket/wringer.
Six guys shoveling snow,

eight pigeons arching,
swooping,

this lazy poet.

Clouds were thick, bitterly
intense, heaving snow, now
empty, thinning. Sun wants

out, its turn
long over-due.

Norma surprises me,
walks through snow bundled
in deep blue coat,

red/white wool cap down
over ears, identical
scarf, mittens, blue corduroy

knickers, light brown
leather boots to knees,
laced; smiles, waves

up to me.

Once said she'd
be there, asked
would I see

her?

I jump up
excited, grin, wave,
want to be out

there with her, together
frolic in snow like
youthful lovers.

Insane asylums full
of poets took themselves
too seriously, forgot

to have fun. *Did*
grab coat, run
through poetry stacks, down

stairs, out door, myself
wide open, ready for
Winter Wonderland.

KITCHEN TABLE, SPRING MORNING

For Norma & Saroyan

Three green apples, two
oranges, three red
tulips, never to know

permanence beneath
gallery lights
in any form,

alive *here* in
All of this
new sun, just for us!

FOR MY SON SAROYAN, ON HIS HIGH SCHOOL GRADUATION, MAY 31ST, 1984 GREENSBORO, NORTH CAROLINA

"The blazing 3 o'clock
sun stares down on
his second-hand

store crib, drying, a
new white." Wrote that
in apprenticeship poem,

1967. Comes to mind now,
Norma and I walking
to your graduation, middle

of third straight week
without rain, temperature
exploding over 90!

Broke today as then.

Adrienne Rich accurate when
she said, "North American
poetry is destined to be

a luxury, a decorative
garnish on the buffet-table
of the university curriculum,

the ceremonial occasion, the
national celebration."

Ground cracked,
hollow, nothing is
lifted.

*

Here, in traditional
setting, school's last
moments of authority,

7th row, 2nd chair from
center aisle, you sit
handsome in borrowed,

rich green gown, mortar-
board gold tasseled, not
trapped by youthful ignorance

anticipating eternal rainbow.

Since small, had a sense
of what was important,
went after it, living

from heart, taking risks.

Now, your turn on platform
to accept Diploma, plus

Outstanding Artist Award

O. Henry Writing Award

In face of affluent
materialistic society
committed to alienating the

importance of artists,
poets, you're ready,
clearly.

This poem begins.

GEM SPA

For Ted Berrigan
1934-1983

Thinking of Ted while
eating breakfast at Gem Spa,
2nd Ave and St. Mark's,

nearly miss all of
beauty walking by
under umbrella.

Not quite!

Enough seen
to say she has
power to take away

misery of January rain
that won't end, but can't
reach my heart because

she was there this once.

NEW YORK CITY MORNING, NOVEMBER 15TH, 1983

For Ted Berrigan
1934-1983

Cold, black, New York City morning,
Saroyan and I after all night drive
from Greensboro to read at Ted's memorial,
happily sit inside enduring '72 Maverick
at curb, 9th street near 2nd, listening
to National Public Radio's homage to Ted.
I'm on it.

Blood moving faster then. Voice
lively to friend, poet.
Sitting *here* now on *his* turf
feeling distinct harmony with him,
son; two easiest guys to love I've known.

Crossed 6th and 1st with two glazed doughnuts,
Village Voice. Knew, understood, in rare way,
raw fact of what it's all about:

those skinny books
we leave behind.

"What strikes the eye hurts. What one hears is a lie."

Ted wrote that.

At St. Mark's, shoulders, sleeves
of old winter coat bulges
from cold rain. Wasn't allowed
to give gifts to Alice, she
and Ted's sons, Anselm, Edmond.
Leave them at entrance
with a coordinator.

Let Anne Waldman know I am there.
Give her inscribed first issue
of *captain may i,* spring, '69,
Ted guest poet.

Not invited to sit
with rest of poets. Don't know
all are sitting together.

Find own place.

Not allowed to read
when turn comes on program.
Person before, immediately
following, read.

Patiently, Saroyan and I wait.
Constant movement in/
out doors, through auditorium.
Voices from loudspeakers
hard to understand. Poets read,
leave. Audience shrinks.
Anne reads, leaves. Others
read. Moving around,
endless.

I want to yell

WHO'S THIS FOR

IT'S TED'S BIRTHDAY

HE'S DEAD

NEVER AGAIN WILL BE HERE

WHY COULDN'T YOU GET

YOUR ACT TOGETHER THIS ONCE

—FOR HIM?

Saroyan chews out a coordinator,
says I'm next.
I'm not.
Longer, we wait.

I'm here, but you won't let me be.

We leave.

Ted, always will have
Special Memories
of *your* turf
Saroyan and I walked.

No one can
take them away.
They're ours for keeps.

IMPERSONATING TED IN WARM MEMORY

For Ted Berrigan
1934-1983

In Brooklyn spring rain everything is possible,
except this time.
Everyone is somewhere else, so I picnic alone
in bed's big middle dreaming of Babe & I
swigging Pepsi & having our picture taken
on the Williamsburg Bridge.

In stagnant summer humidity,
back where I belong,
dead flys on the window ledge
pile up.
My energy enrages others silently.

In fall, time out to not fool around.
Final storing of reserves for winter
when single-step-at-a-time forward
determines survival.
There, that said, makes this poem serious,
if you believe me.

It's 3:26 A.M. in NYC's January heart
in alley off 6th at St. Mark's,
bedded into her bags and rags,
what does this rosey old lady face grinning see?
Oh, the pleasures of being down, but not out!

LATE FALL, '84

Brilliant sun pours in
glaring against this
desk top.

Leaves, deformed,
scrape against sidewalk,
prance momentarily.

Again! Again! I have
begged Christ for mercy.
This physical pain,

ferocity without relief.

Once I died.

He stopped me, holding up hand
like a traffic cop,
not allowing freedom
feeble body wanted.

Soon, ragged chunks of winter.
Press on in poverty's skeleton.

YEAR END NOTES '84

Boys learning violent
domination with poseable
war figures from cartoons, movies,
videos, magazines, tv news.

Girls learning passive
consumerism from Big-Breasted
Barbie, her wardrobe, commercials,
ads EVERYWHERE!

*

Low-key image of youth—
lack of commitment
developing future role
of abspestos zombie?

*

Adults inarticulate, uninvolved,
watching, hiding, flitting about,
concerned only with own forgetable
tiny tasks, conveniences, comforts.

*

In demand: soft violence—like

drinking self to death

o.d.ing

quietly going crazy.

*

Tired yet of talking
to each other with only
t-shirt fronts, bumper stickers?

*

Flash of disc camera immortalizes
your life to Christ's tearful eye.

SOUND

Not a woman lovingly
whispering my name
through the sky
but a lady bug
walking eye-level
on the other side
of this screen.

IN A DREAM

Last night,
sleeping,

in a dream,
a woman
gave *me* Love!

Waking,
exalted from pain, suffering!

(Soaring in silent room,
small tick for me
in ticking of time?)

Know, life lived
from heart, experiences
more than what wanted.

Know, still
want a woman
not afraid of love.

COORDINATED BRAS, GIRDLES

Womens league cake sale
given in coordinated
bras, girdles. Time
moves around them
like thick July humidity.

All subscribe to
"Hands On Art,"
by mail. Unexplained
bursts of activity.
Custom-designed eye thrills?

Need more than
poking holes in air
with finger, saying,
"Look, see what I did."

"Say it in neon, Baby,"
freon salesman urges,
"just sign the
white slip."

Instead, begin constant
pacing, bent forward, searching
no-wax tile floors
for invisible answers?

Meaning here, if any,
less when compared to
jubilant witnesses,
Mississippi tent revival,
1983.

42½

For Federico Fellini

Tall, skinny guy
rides old, dull,
skinny bicycle
on narrow sidewalk,
long, thin cigar
straight out
from tight, lipless mouth.

Short crippled woman
on crooked wooden crutches
stops,
pulls crutches
tight against self,
to let him pass.

He doesn't acknowledge
courteous gesture.

She, with angry thrust of arm
toward peddling arrogance,
fist clenched, slashes air
with straight-up middle finger.

Fat, peroxided blond
in worn, red boots,
dark purple, baggy slacks,
full length, phoney sable,

wrestles crutches from her,
embraces them as though
dancing partner, glides
into alley.

Legless beggar lifts
cripple onto
decaying skateboard,
heads down 9th
passed hubcaps, rats,
too short for Michelangelo sculpture.

WATCHING IT RAIN FROM A SECOND FLOOR DOWNTOWN WINDOW

Below,
the world All Bright
singular
carrousels.

Look!
Three are opening
at once!

Above,
in the clouds,
the engine

makes it All
work.

PENNY, THIS ONE'S FOR YOU

Abused throughout
childhood, youth. Anything
left?

"Listen, Creep,
I burn with life—I
care about a lot—I can
write poems."

Always looks like
she wants to be
somewhere else. Endless,

demons over shoulder.
Something in bottom of
bucket for her?

Yellow daffodils
in clear glass jar
on window sill,

cold,

grey,

early spring morning,
first offering
to new season.

OLD, USED, TRUE

My friend Agnes scrubs
the pots and frying pans
at the cafeteria on 11th,
tells me, "It's in the arms
—the legs last longest
—my life is in these arms
—as long as they hold up,
I hold up."

*

At the 24-hour cafe on fourth
Burger short orders,
the regular drunks and whores
tell new customers stories
about when he was Head chef
for Joe Louis and Rocky Marciano.

Short, wirey, bald,
he tells a new fan,
"Yah, I'm gonna beat death
—me n' these arms
—yah, we're gonna turn it
into chopped liver,"
grins like he really believes it.

*

"Blond dreams is for kids,"
Sweet Sue, the 76 year-old candy lady
tells me from her booth in city hall.
"The ones who don't outgrowum'
go batty, though they look all right
—but to hearum' talk,
you know they got on the wrong ride.

"They're livin' inside their tv's
—hypnotized by all that
blond melodrama crap
—they believe it
—think it's gonna happen to them
—think an everlastin' magic wand
gonna come right out
and take away their boredom

—their isolation
—their wasted lives
—their ugly, wasted lives."

*

The old who won't
enter nursing homes

The old who won't
feed pigeons in the park

The old who won't
play checkers in the park

The old who won't
move to Florida

The old who won't
accept 10% discounts

The old who don't
feel guilty stealing food
so they can survive

The old who haven't
suddenly "found" Christ
because there isn't
anything else to do

The old who don't
believe silence is golden

The old who don't
believe silence is strength

The old who won't
quit because it's expected

The old who know
trying is the one thing
we have left

The old who live in single rooms
with a hot plate
share the toliet down the hall
and have a framed Kodak snapshot
of their wedding

About as many
staying out there doing it
as good poems never read.

UPON RECEIVING A REJECTION LETTER FROM *THE AMERICAN POETRY REVIEW* FOR NINE POEMS I HAD THERE FOR *FOURTEEN-AND-A-HALF* MONTHS

Dear Jim,

Sorry to take so long with these, which have
strong perceptual moments but which, to me, seem
to have reduced your experiences too far into a
kind of primitive statement. But thanks for sending
them in.

Sincerely,

Steve Berg

Dear Steve,

I was going to send you a finger,
but the shops were closed.

Jim Humphrey

T.S. ELIOT GOES UNDERGROUND

Crowded subway station, 57th
at 7th, Saroyan and I
waiting for St. Mark's ride

to take us closer
to Ted. Short, scrawny guy,
Army jacket, jeans,

hawks

"GET YOUR T.S. ELIOT POEMS

HERE

DIME-A-TIME!"

Rips pages from
old, cloth book.
Sells two.

Someone says

"Who was he?"

Woman my age
yells

"ANY WORDS THERE
STILL TRUE?"

I holler back
"WERE THEY EVER?"

READING POEMS IN A STORE FRONT CHURCH

Reading perfectly
to empty, ragged, folding chairs
in rough rows.

One raw ceiling light
burning on and on. Something
twisting above its tortured
plaster, layers of paint?

Wrenching sounds of
jazz Master Muddy Waters?

Can see brown articulate fingers
squeezing plaster, paint,
like old flowers.

Washed in the blood
of Jesus, not to die,
lost in the night.

GREAT IS MEDIOCRE, OR LESS

Modern America rides
constant crest for

new novelties to kill
time with, reducing

everything to lowest
common denominator

so nobody will
feel inferior.

WARNING

Most go old finally
with habits fastened
securely in head,
heart no more
than dried muscle.

Heaven not aimed
at old folks with regrets,
who, when younger,
didn't obey simple direction
of the heart:
to love with *all* its might.
Can't now be made up
in prayer.

LASTING

1

9th floor *here*
in library last night
building empty except

hiding young apprentice
writer, plunged through
locked window
                    to death.

Cleaning lady said,
"He looked like
broken doll all smeared

with lipstick." People
who would otherwise
walk by, stop, now

look up, point to
busted window, a few,
lips move, silently.

2

Takes time
to get it
right inside

yourself, if
you want to
last. Easy

not to; courage,
risk, more than
meets the eye,

more to it
than recognition, or
lack of it.

Truth
of myself, all
that counts.

Slowly,

am learning what
it takes
to last.

LIFE-LONG CARNIVAL TROUPER

For Red

Harder to enter
mornings; this one
for instance, could be

any one, all alike
except for tiny feeling
remains inside.

A feeling Red never
tried to explain. There
from when a kid, went

to first carnival,
now gives him
necessary stubborness.

Clay sticks to boots
from dogged drizzle
as he makes way

to tilt-a-whirl to
weld cracked safety bar
on number two car.

Eight rides left, three
games of chance, one small
trailer for popcorn, soda.

Old, all of it, broken; paint
pale, gouged, light sockets
empty, shows first.

Will be gone
soon enough, forever
dead to the world.

Still time left
for him to say
to worker new in spring,

and me to hear,
"Don't get married, Kid
—you know what a woman wants

—to get pregnant,
keep you on the road
and collecting your checks

—the edge gets close quick enough
without putting up with
her sloppy body and dumb mouth

—remember that."

Summer is now, will change
to something else
soon enough, indifferent to us.

Red, you listened to heart,
obeyed it all your life.
You might be last

American Hero.

Maybe more of what
is actual will be said
in the silence you leave.

THE OLD WOMAN ON THE FRONT PORCH

Always sitting in the
old rocker on the sagging
front porch in the same
wrinkled grey dress, faded
burgundy shawl. Brushed grey hair

to shoulders, thick, neat; once
attractive face, deep brown eyes,
gone to an unchanging blank stare.
Never speaking.

Nearly two years, I have seen her
this way as I walk by, sensing
my mother looks like her.

A year ago, near the side
of the house, she stood
in the mess of rotting tomatoes
and carnival colored zinnias and
marigolds of fall's short days,
crying at the street

"No one feels another's suffering,

only their death!"

Winter, spring, summer, she
stayed on the porch, staring,
silent. Today the sun falls
on her in the rotting vegetables
and bright flowers, once more
lamenting to the indifferent street.

POSSIBLE TO BE SIXTEEN AGAIN?

For Carole Harsted

1

Possible to be sixteen again
without daily horrors from
sadist stepfather scarring
me for life, living in

constant guilt, living in
constant fear I will be
punished for EVERYTHING
I do?

Especially now, Oh
especially now, in this
high school talking to the
sophomore literature class;

old chipped blackboard, cloth
erasers, sweet aroma of peanut
butter and jelly sandwiches
through wrinkled brown sacks,

the particular sound of a
single-zipper notebook opening.

Alive in me as she was at
the Sophomore Winter Sock Hop,
blond Carole in white angora
sweater, tight grey wool skirt

to middle of firm, shapely calves,
dancing together forever to the
Four Aces singing "Love Is
A Many Splendored Thing."

2

To be born again at sixteen,
given parents who could
give me love, guidance, allowed
to develop abilities, allowed

to see how far I *could* go; *not*
forced to survive in the
unredeeming street, my heart outside
my filthy coat; damned to be

the eternal victim.

Now at age forty-six, still
living in poverty's skeleton,
I can make *clear* acknowledgment
of Worth through the guilt, fear.

Can also say without dread
of becoming like him,
stepfather rages in my head,
demanding his evil be obeyed.

OHHHHHHHHH! To have been allowed
youth's technicolored dreams,
cinemascope pleasures, plans!

Surely,
I'd never become a poet.

BEAUTIFUL HOUSEWIVES AND CAREER WOMEN!

BEAUTIFUL HOUSEWIVES AND CAREER WOMEN
EVERYWHERE IN SIGHT! Could be surrounded
if I keep moving with them.

Enters me: can each give, still knows how,
understands importance, strength in such
generosity?

Giving more than meals,
clean house; becoming more than new job
in trousers, pin-striped suits.

Imagination, sensitivity alive enough
to give self from heart?

Possible, everything
but a heart beat.

Suddenly want to yell:

CAN ANYONE GIVE ANYMORE!

Sometimes, wish it did
amount to only reproduction,
wanting, feeling no more, no less

than person next to me.

CELEBRATING MY COURAGE TO KEEP TRYING

Could write about snow
got during night brightening
constant grey days

to walk around in.
Tiny yellow flowers locked
in ice, women sexy in

long coats, hair down back,
scarfs to knees, boots looking
up under all of it.

See them all, want
them all. Love two, know
one. Lucky you, if you do.

Car slides on ice, slaps
stoplight, draws crowd.
Everyone excited, jabbering

at once. Sirens, flashing
lights. Two kids, 11 or 12
with double-dip

strawberry cones, walk by,
ignore exaggerated commotion.
He puts the ice cream

against tip of
his nose, cone straight out, looks

cross-eyed. She giggles. I
smile, realizing just then,
the miracle is coming back

from the last war alive,
repairing again, still wanting
joy in simple things.

18 DEGREES

Sun, small white glaze
somewhere behind
cement clouds.

Snow, grey, jagged,
pitted black,
exhibiting torn newspapers,
piles of dogshit,
busted booze bottles:

our country's most constant
public art
signifying the human condition.

But wait!
Something Bright is happening!
A pale, skinny man, eyes sunk back,
but smiling,
dressed only in a yellow short-sleeved shirt,
summer trousers—bright green,
rolled to the knees,
the woman with him,
pale, skinny, eyes sunk back,
is dressed in sleeveless pink blouse,
white shorts, sandals,
is smiling and waving
as she and the man walk through the ugliness,
taking turns carrying a large rectangular painting
from K Mart or Woolworth's at $14.99
of a big, lazy, foamy ocean wave
beneath bright, warm sky,
a second away from kissing
an empty, sandy beach.

In this city, January, 1983,
unemployment is over 14 percent!
People are desperate, impoverished,
forced to live in alleys, doorways,
beneath bridges, in cardboard boxes,
people with no more hope to use up,
walking, standing, squating,
dying invisible deaths.

The dead don't see
that the man and woman
are trying to make them laugh,
are trying bring life
back into them.

The dead don't see
that to do what the man and woman are doing
is rooted in deep suffering
as they are suffering.

The dead won't laugh.
They only see that life is over for them,
so they yell,
"YOU CRAZY OR SOMETHIN'!"
"GO ON BEAT IT!"
"WE DON'T NEED NO LOONEYS HERE!"

In a few moments, the man and woman are gone.
The isolation has been kept intact.
There is a silent pride in this,
as there is a silent longing in each of them
for their final death.

FORGOTTEN

L. Rasmusson, Photographer
hardly recognizable painted
words on single
display window facing street.

Under dust, dead
insects, bowed against
window's backdrop, black
and white photographs,
some indistinguishable.

Army private, arm
around waist of
Dream-Come-True
in Sunday's church dress.

Old woman holding
sign: "I AM ABLE
WORK IS WHAT I WANT
WHO WILL HELP ME?"

Line of people
fishing off bridge,
tuba player, four
children in a
school bus, janitor
mopping, six dancers,
two department store
clerks, cheerleader
splitting the air.

In door window,
single piece of
tape reamins holding
typed sheet of paper,
yellowed, corners curling:

Closed
due to funeral of
Mr. L. Rasmusson.

The date is not given.

FOR THE NYC SUBWAY GRAFFITI WRITERS

2 a.m., secret ways
around barbed wire,
watch dogs, into
subway yards where

Gallant steel awaits
oranges, reds, purples
and beyond to become
Emblazoned Fast Art;

Rocking the city
with *your* name
on a train, not weak hold

of language deteriorating
ahead of unthinkable,
as archaic city bosses
want public to believe.

Julia True or False,
Taki 183, K 161, Seem, Mare,
Trap, Zephyr, Michael Stewart,
all of you, each,

commanding light in
dark with Monday morning
Hits until you vanish,
but will *never, never die.*

SKINNY, TOUGH POET

For Jesse

Skinny, tough poet,
lives in slums—Chicago,

sometimes KC, Omaha.
Unpublished,

doesn't expect to be.
Knows *his* life *is*

all *he's* got. Laughs
"name" poets off

for being cheap, allowing
demanding powers

to display them
as window dressing.

Says there are
a couple good ones,

won't name. Asks
if he's being screened

for tv game show.
Laughs. Leaves.

POETRY OFFICER

Her own
eye to

see never
occured to

her. Affected
pale complexion,

emphasizing delicacy.
Only dream,

preserve faded
gentility. Life's

work, tidy,
polite poetry

to rule
always.

SONS AND FATHERS

Laid off from the cotton mill five years,
the son sits on the cement steps
at his front door across the street
from this window 18-20 hours a day,
seven days a week with coffee and cigarettes,
staring into the street, face of pain
but of little experience or purpose.

When the mill closed four years ago,
the father employed there forty-eight years,
began sitting on the front steps next to him,
thinking himself gutted flesh, ignoring the son.

As the months tightened into a year,
the father withdrew deeper into himself,
was put into a straight jacket
and taken to the madhouse.

He died there a year ago.

Last Friday, the son ran up and down the street
holding a big stew pot over his head yelling,
PROTECT YOURSELF!
WE'RE ALL GOING TO DIE FROM METAL FALLOUT!
No one paid any attention, not even
the beer-sucking dirt-yard squatters.
Soon, his legs gave out
and he quit, threw the pot at a house
and went back to the front steps.

There is a way to keep yourself
from becoming your father.

I had two of them to defeat.

First five years of my life, 1939-44,
blood father was a gung-ho marine sergeant
who found glory in WW II's South Pacific,
divorcing mom at war's end
for fucking another guy
who beat me the first time we met,
married mom and kept on beating me
almost every day for the next twelve years.

Twice, I ran away to dad's house
but he wouldn't let me in, saying
he had two fine sons to raise.

At work (he was a cattle salesman
at the stockyards, as his father was)
he told his buddies,
"Jimmie was a mistake—you know
the kid you didn't want to have,
but were stuck with.
Naw, he doesn't come around anymore
—heard his old man crippled him,
and kicked him out."

There is a way to keep yourself
from becoming your father.

Keeping your heart alive.
Living from there.

Determined to make me jelly, father and stepfather
implanted the depth of love I feel and give.
They embedded the poet in me.

Tonight they took the son away,
while this son sits here
making another comeback
in complete surrender to the written word,
its Strengths, its Joys, its Satisfactions,

its Cleansing.

FOR RICHARD HUGO

1923-1982

The bombs from World War II
kept killing the roses.
Nothing would stop the guilt.
Nightmares kept the bottle near.

The girl from '39
wouldn't come back
not one day older,
holding out her arms.

We had in common
alcohol,
the guts to
quit it. Talked

about it when we met,
February '75, New York City.
Told you *The Hilltop* was
my favorite poem about

alcohol's deep loneliness,
pain, guilt. You shrugged,
laughed,
reminding me more of a

jolly candy store owner
than a poet on tour,
spreading the word.

"It's all there," I said,
"in 27 lines—the reinforcement
of everything necessary to keep
a man drowning in the sauce."

You smiled,
and with a single swoop
of an arm,
waved the words away.

You won, Richard!
You beat the bottle, the ghosts,
sticking it out to the end.

You gave us some good poems,
a few are great.
This one is for you,
a poem as farewell drink,

and a minute of silence.

PARLOR POETESS SPEAKING TO GARDEN CLUB

"A number of
my pō-əms have
come from Heaven.

The retina splitting
what can't be seen,
dividing us from

The Holy Grail,
will be theme
for my next pō-əm.

But how to
frame it—set it
in playful typography."

STUDYING GREAT WRITERS

What does it mean,
this old, frail guy in child's stocking cap,
torn jacket, gloveless,
15 degrees,
picking up small tree branches, twigs,
dropping them onto an old hill sled,
the sides, front, back, built high
with chicken wire.

What does it mean,
so many university students
studying Dostoyevsky, Villon, Charles Dickens,
Solzhenitsyn, Thomas Merton, Saint Augustine,
who do not see the old man,
though they walk by him.

What does it mean
when *she* walks out on *you,*
and you get drunk, miss classes for two days,
including the one on great writers,
find a whore, swearing silent revenge.

You stay drunk and miss another two days of classes,
desperately wanting to climb into
the bar's Budweiser sign,
where you can stay drunk and hidden forever.

Too much puking forces you to sleep it off,
sober up, return to classes,
quickly falling back into your old routine
with a new co-ed,
not learning anything from Dostoyevsky, Villon,
Dickens, Solzhenitsyn, Merton, Augustine,
or from your own mistakes.

What does it mean
when *he* walks out on *you,*
and you keep it all inside:
the loss, the betrayal, the guilt, the anger,
pretending calmness,
continuing to study, going to classes,
including the one on great writers,
your friends admiring your strength,
your control.

Nine or ten days later, in the cafeteria,
you bite a small bone
in your tuna sandwich, and want
with all of your broken-hearted being,
to SCREAM,
THROW THE SANDWICH AT THE PASSING MALE STUDENT,
but don't because your in a public place;
people might think you're crazy.

Silently, you take the bone from the sandwich,
lay it on the side of the plate
and take a bite of salad,
as though nothing had ever bothered you
in your entire life.

What does it mean
when a male student studying great writers
is asked by an old derelict for a quarter
or a buck,
and doesn't try to understand
that no one grows up intending to be a beggar;
laughs snidely, says, "Beat it, Creep!"
and hurridly moves away,
as though poverty is a catchable disease.

What does it mean
when a female student studying great writers
is asked directions by an old, ugly woman,
who repeatedly needs to have them explained.
Exasperated, the student rushes off,
thinking her stupid,

not realizing it wasn't the slowness
that caused anger,
but being *old,* being *ugly.*
Not ready yet to admit that *her* face,
her body, will lose its attractivness,
its tightness;
will go soft, *will* wrinkle.

You're fools!
You're going to make it worse
than it is
wanting only what's safe, immediate,
accepting role of inferior,
ignoring the importance of risk,
sacrifice, loss, endurance, truth,
Great writers have left us.

WHAT SHE DID TO ME

Surely, a few
hands and hearts
embracing somewhere
in this country

beyond

churches

hospitals

mortuaries

and meaning it.

You came into
my heart today
and didn't know it.

In a
look
arrived

making me want
to comb my hair
right in the heart

of January's raw rain.

My heart's an
open kid, lets me
sing out!

FOR BEVERLY KNUDSON

Died July 11th, 1984

At anti-nuclear and
acid-rain rallies, she
chanted "Nothing human

is bad unless it's
unkind or violent."

Turbulant 60's
Rock & Roll absorbed
old, moveable Greyhound

she lived alone in
surrounded by crudely let-
tered magic marker words

against rainbow metal
announcing

Real Name For
Magic Is Strength

The Spirit Requires
Variety

Truth Is Simple
When Nothing to Hide

Speak The Truth
And Chain The Devil

To the world, the bus's dull
lengths proclaimed in Large,
Bright, Juicy letters

FOR THE SHEER WONDER OF IT ALL

Found dead. Butchered,
inside the bus.

When we see death, how
privately real our own
lives become, clearly

knowing, at least for
that moment, how we
should live.

FOR BEVERLY KNUDSON'S MOM AND DAD, MARGARET AND RUE

Their whole lives had been given
to speaking out for the poor.
Last winter in South Dakota

Rue said, "See closer the horrors
of Native Americans. Live with them,
eat at their table what the

government gives them. What difference
does it make how much I see, feel,
say to you?"

In spring in Mississippi, Margaret said

> "BREAK YOUR BALLS!
> BREAK YOUR BACK!
> BREAK YOUR LUCK!
>
> IF YOU ARE DESERTED,
> FOLLOW THE DESERTED CHRIST!
>
> CUT IT ANYWAY YOU WANT,
> BUT QUIT BREAKING *YOUR* HEART!
> FEEL THE SUN TRYING TO
>
> BUST IN! BEGIN AGAIN!
> -*NOT* BACKWARD TO WHAT OTHERS
> WRONGLY MADE YOU THINK YOU ARE!
>
> HERE! NOW! TRUST IN YOURSELF,
> FOR YOURSELF!
>
> In kindness, in kindness."

Her daughter's murder was
too deep a shock. In bed to die from stroke,
tubes up her nose, in her mouth, body grey,

sight, voice, hearing gone. Will never know
Rue sits at the window dying a suicide
never to be recorded.

SATURDAY NIGHT WITH GUS & ADA

"ADA! YOU GOT MORALS
OF A TWO BUCK WHORE!"
Gus yells while repeatedly
slugging her.

She doesn't scream or cry
anymore. Just takes it.

Ada, in the beginning
were you ignorant golden wheat
before the self-serving
reaper's blade?

Oh, Ada, were you ever
lost in a sea of swirling
white gowns under the brilliant
fantasy chandelier?

Hey, Gus, did you learn
violent domination as a kid
playing G.I. Joe, or from
violent tv: "The bullets

tore into his shoulder and
stomach, his lungs burning,
the crowd cheering wildly!"

Is that you, Gus, the hero
of the invisible audience?

"WHAT IS THIS SHIT!" Gus demands,
grabbing the paper from my hand.

"A POEM!" Ada screams trying to
tear it from his grip, "A POEM
ABOUT *UGLY, UGLY* US!"

He holds it above his
head, says "This don't
look like no poem!"

It's not, I tell him. It's
a secret code.

"I see," he says, picks Ada up
as if a rag doll, throws her
into tenament building hallway,
locks door, sits down

at kitchen table, begins
reading it.

THE ONLY HOPE I HAVE LEFT

March 7th, 1983

Last night, two blocks over,
a jealous, sadistic son-of-a-bitch
tortured his 10 year-old step-son
to death
for being an A student.

Last night, behind the house next door,
a jealous, sadistic son-of-a-bitch
blew his 17 year-old son's head off
while working out.
He had believed he would run the marathon
in the '84 Olympics.

Last night, at county, the doctors told me
I had intestinal cancer and would be dead
in less than six months.

The two dead boys were the lucky ones.
They had gotten out of the horror show early.
I knew I wouldn't die.
Deep, constant suffering
isn't meant to kill me.

The only hope I have left
is after I'm dead,
through my poems,
my life will begin.

FOR MARILYN MONROE

Nights too dark, too
long, too often. Nothing

left in head, heart
to live with. Step-

father's cruelty from
childhood always haunting

her. Final whimper, a
hopeless prayer, same

one always pleaded
with him, "What do

you want?" Dying that way;
his ultimate victory.

WORKING CLASS WOMAN

"This is Monday late
—one, two, three, four
working days left this week,"
woman near 60 says to no one
while opening something or other.

FOR MAY VAN VOOREN

Died 1979

She spent final months
in old stuffed chair
next to street window

in living room of white-
painted, depression-built
house, Hazleton, Iowa.

Real doilies—cotton
crochet, on the chairs,
couch, end tables. Framed

pictures on walls. Across
from her, Jesus rising,
dried palm leaves curling

above Him. Kodak snapshot
of she and husband Art,
dead ten years, on table

beside her cluttered
with small objects, pieces,
accumulated, always there,

bringing pleasure to her
last days stronger than cancer.

Hot, bright August afternoon,
1979, the last time I saw her.

A tall, big woman, years
in sixties, healthy appearance,
voice deep, strong, told me

I would be okay, life not
as serious
as I made it out to be.

That she cared at all
was miracle enough. She,
too, had sadistic stepfather

beat, tortured her when child.
Completely, I respected her,
sensed her honest substance,

witnessed strength in ways
developed only by determination
to endure, contribute.

In new winter, she died,
I like to think without fear
stepfather was in shadows

waiting, set to punish her.

The life-long necessity to
rise above him, his monsterous
acts the last time,

not occurring to her.

I SIT IN THIS TINY ROOM

For Charles Bukowski

I sit in this tiny room
in the city's underbelly
making another come back,
legs wrapped, upper and lower back
in braces, cane at my side,
arms held up to this typer by books,
ears infected, throat infected,
pneumonia trying to suck me
into the indifferent ground.

I sit in this tiny room
making another come back
while thousands of mediocre poets
believing Eliot, Auden and Ashbery
are the way, teach, live in fine
houses and apartments, give readings
telling everyone what they want to hear,
offending no one,
just like all uninteresting people,
whether poet, insurance salesperson or
high-tech promo rep.

I sit in this tiny room
making another comeback
while thousands of mediocre poets
frantically compete to be published
by the few large trade presses,
keeping alive the accepted myth
that poetry is written only by
tenured English professors and wealthy heirs.

I sit in this tiny room
having made come backs from
terminal cancer, alcoholism,
paralysis, a sadistic stepfather,
passive mother, deep emotional scars,
rubbing my soul with 50s Rock N Roll
on a little grey mono tape player,
while thousands of mediocre poets
unmarked by pain or suffering,
continue the reflection
of their uninteresting lives
in all of that intense writing
about nothing much.

MERRY CHRISTMAS, JACKSON LIBRARY, YOU'VE BEEN GOOD TO ME!

Written twelve poems
worth thirty-seven
pages in last

twenty days, including
six days off too
sick to work. Would like

one more before putting
energy into Christmas,
four days away.

Can't get it, can't
get the juices
juicing, the words

wording. That's okay.
Twenty years, I was
alcoholic,

six short poems
in a year,
remarkable.

*

Two boys, eleven
or twelve, walk
nearby, through

the poetry stacks
killing time, loudly
calling out book numbers,

slapping them. Do they know
it's books of poems
they're playing with,

know there are *living*
poets, will ever know it?

*

Norma tip-toes
to carrel. I am
looking out window,

lazily watching grey
squirrel circle rusted
trash can once,

twice, lope away. Norma
stands folded 3x5
pink card on top

narrow ledge separates
this carrel from
one adjoining,

tip-toes away.

When I turn, looking
straight at me are
the handwritten red words

MERRY CHRISTMAS, LOVER!

Risks worth it in
possibilities this
life is awakened to

by simple words from
the heart, human,
impermanent.

CHRISTMAS CARD
FROM MY SON SAROYAN

Dear Jim

A new limo can be rented anytime,
a great poem can never be.

Love, Saroyan

KEEPING BLOOD GOING THIRD CONSECUTIVE WINTER WITHOUT HEAT IN THE HOUSE

Nothing lovelier through

street window than

Bright Sun in woman's

natural blond hair except

sun through

bedroom window &

blond in bed
with me.

*

American Poet: separate
existence in
fragmentary way, mostly

hanging on.

Rest

of it Leap of Faith.

*

I wished her
here
she
went where

*

Someday will have
neon sign in window

POETRY READING

blinking on, off,
like 24-hr-cafe sign,
the only light

to lessen grief.

THE BEATEN CAN'T STAND

If it's not busted mufflers on
ragged trucks and old, wasted
cars, its police and ambulance
sirens screaming down this street
of alcoholics, drug addicts,
the illiterate, the homeless,
leaning against abandoned store fronts,
standing slumped in grey doorways,
trapped by forces they can't defeat.

If it's not mothers screaming
at screaming babies, big kids
screaming at little kids, A.M.
radios screaming, fathers screaming
they can't take anymore, it's
dozens of cats tormenting the few
remaining dogs, it's blackbirds
and crows screaming from dead trees,
dirt yards, and from piles of rotting garbage.

Jail, county hospital, state madhouse,
the ways out.

This is what was intended.

This is the excrement of man's greed, power.

History declares this street will be forgotten,
like an old wound,
replaced by high-rises, condos, indoor shops,
only to have moved to another street,
nearer your street.

HEROES ARE HARD TO FIND

Sheets of rain won't quit
on a hot July afternoon.
Nine kids playing

across the street
around a downed
tenement building.

Slushy mud balls
slide down shirts,
arms, jeans.

Little girls, boys, shirtless,
arms, fingers, thin,
stretched

high as they will go,
dancing, running, squealing.

An older girl, 12 or so,
head back,
long brown hair straight down

dripping,
legs straight out,
glides in a swing

hooked to a beam,
innocent as the Virgin Mary.

Not sweet redemption
of Heaven;
renewing life

on earth
for themselves, for me.

STILL TRYING

What are the words,
meaning there,
when rage held in?

Shrill, amplified guitars
from the mill house
behind this one,
AM radio rock slamming in
from the front,
have used me up.

Mind sucked into them.
Words newly written
don't do, only say.

Want to float away
with firm-thighed girl
suddenly remembered from month ago,
passed in a glance.

Instead hear radios blare:
"SUBSTANCE OR SPECTACLE!
THE FUTURE BELONGS TO WHOEVER
CAN BUY IT!"

"AND THE POOR MAN'S WISDOM IS DESPISED!"
I shout, vanishing from all of it

into the hot shower: 1968,
Moody Blues insist
Thinking is the best way to travel.

Still broke
as I was then; still
riding my mind, know
I'm doing more than
putting time in before dying.

JAMES HUMPHREY was born in Sioux City, Iowa, February 20th, 1939. From age 5 to 16, he was forced to live with a sadistic stepfather and passive mother. They lived in poverty, often moving throughout the Midwest. Big enough physically at 16, he beat up the six-foot stepfather and left, never to return. Not having a guardian, he wasn't allowed to continue high school. The next winter, in poor health, living in Iowa in bushes and cardboard boxes, not expecting to last until spring, he wrote his first poem, *A Fallen Man Searching,* which appeared unchanged in his chapbook *In Tribute To Survivors* (1984). The constant physical, mental and emotional abuse beaten and tortured into him when a child and young teen, the severe circumstances *and* reason for writing his first poem: "The intention was to define myself in a single piece before starving or freezing to death," set the foundation for the raw emotions he bravely enters in his daily living and daring simplicity when he writes. With the maturing of his writing, to say his poems are direct, honest and personal, is secondary. Without trying to do so, he has set a new standard in American poetry long overdue: to discover your heart, open it, and live from it with all of your might.

At age 34 he became a college student for the first time, entering Brown University, graduating with distinction two-and-a-half years later with an MA in Creative Writing.

For the last five years he has lived in the South where all of these poems were written. Living in Columbia, North Carolina since July '85, his wife Norma is the Librarian for the Tyrrell County Public Library, and he is Poet-In-Residence at Lawrence Academy, Merry Hill, North Carolina. Their son Saroyan (named after William) has been on his own since graduating from high school in '84. He lives in Charlotte, goes to college full-time studying fine art and advertising design as well as being a full-time staff writer for *Grand National Scene* , a weekly newspaper covering Winston Cup Grand National stock car racing.